The Best-Kept Career Secret

The Best-Kept Career Secret: Professional Sales

Bob Thomas

MIRACLE PRESS

"If it's a hit—it's a MIRACLE!"

To C. B. Buchanan

One of the best sales consultants
Los Angeles has ever had

Miracle Press, LLC
P.O. Box 20787
Carson City, Nevada 89721
775.884.2553

©2006 Miracle Press

First printing 2006

Printed in the United States of America

Cover Design
Doug Hesseltine, Hesseltine & DeMason, Ann Arbor, Michigan

Editorial/Production
Christina Bych, **aatec publications**, Ann Arbor, Michigan

Library of Congress Control Number: 2006920283

ISBN 13: 978-0-9777029-0-9
ISBN 10: 0-9777029-0-1

Contents

Foreword

Professional salespeople are the unsung heroes of our free market, private enterprise economy.

Bob Thomas brings this fact home to college and university students poised on the threshold of the professional marketplace. Then he tells them how to make those critical first steps in his handbook *The Best-Kept Career Secret: Professional Sales.*

Thomas once again addresses a commonplace of the American economic scene with uncommonly direct insights and refreshing advice and counsel, as he did in *The Fail-Proof Enterprise.*

He has reconnected the need for a solid education—a general liberal arts education—with the practical wisdom of the free market economy. He does this by investing our uniquely American liberal studies philosophy with a mission of liberating people to find their own self-transcendant purposes.

The reader of this handbook will learn that to stay the college and university course all the way to a four-year degree is to remain on track to realize the American Dream.

Bob Thomas is the embodiment of what he writes. He inspires by his example, as well as by his words.

He has set the groundwork that should lead to the establishment of professional sales as a college major in its own right.

Dr. Jefferson Allen Stewart
Chairman, National Advisory
Council of the American Society
for Competitiveness

Preface

This book is a compendium of my forty-six years of experience in *the most exciting and rewarding career imaginable.*

My mission in introducing you to this career is to perhaps save you as I was saved. If you are now in college there is the possibility that you may be confused, skeptical, or having doubts about how you will make your living following graduation. Are you majoring in the ideal field? Does your major offer a good means of making a living? Is your major field overcrowded? These questions need to be answered.

You may even be contemplating dropping out of school in favor of finding a job. That would be the dumbest thing you could possibly do.

I have a much better idea.

This career we're talking about—professional sales—doesn't require any specific major . . . *as long as you have your bachelor's degree*. That is a must.

Take your time to digest the following information. Let these chapters open doors you never thought of looking behind, doors perhaps you never knew existed. Your imagination is about to be tweaked, your knowledge broadened.

After reading this little book, should you decide to put my knowledge and experience to use in your behalf, I am confident that the benefits will far outweigh the effort.

Bob Thomas

CHAPTER ONE

YOUR CAREER
THE BIG DECISION

Are you thinking about dropping out of college?

DON'T DO IT!

I am about to give you the best reason you will ever find to remain in school until you get your degree. I am going to introduce you to one of the most exciting and satisfying careers there is—that is, if you have what it takes.

- •Are you thinking of changing your major?
- •Are you not sure what to do after you graduate?

That's okay. The exclusive career I'm referring to rarely calls for a specific major—but it does require at least a bachelor's degree.

What career am I talking about?

Professional Sales.

No, not retail sales. *Professional sales.*

Professional salespeople are college graduates who sell goods, services, and ideas to other professionals.

I am about to challenge you in a most provocative way. However, to be fair to yourself you must be open-minded: Dispense with any preconceived notions you have about sales.

That said, I must add that not everyone is qualified to practice this profession, not everyone has the right combination of skills and aptitudes. But those who do, and who pursue this career, will be rewarded monetarily and aesthetically beyond their dreams.

Let's talk about your college major.

Beginning about 1946, when we GIs were returning home from World War II, we attended college in droves because Uncle Sam was paying for most of it through the GI Bill. That's when a college education began to emerge as a necessity for success, and not, as it had been, a pastime for wealthy kids and a training ground for the intellectual elite. Prior to then, a college or university education was pretty much reserved for those who *knew* they were going to be doctors, engineers, lawyers, scientists, accountants, educators—or perennial students. The idea of getting a college degree as a "union card" for entry into the higher echelons of business, commerce, and the public sector wasn't the norm because in those days employers hired high school graduates and trained them for white collar jobs.

Today we have the other extreme. Higher education is now one of the biggest businesses in our nation. Yes, it is truly a business because it takes money in exchange for services rendered. Non-profit status doesn't change anything. In education, funds accumulated over and above expenses (profits) are banked for future use. In the private sector, profits, after taxes, are often distributed to stockholder-owners. I am perfectly content with higher education being a growing, successful business. Today, education is sold to us by everybody—our parents, our friends, our teachers, and our future employers—as being our primary salvation economically, asethetically, and philosophically. And a good education is all of those things.

Because the pendulum has swung so far in that direction, we now have students entering college without the slightest idea of what they want to do as a career following graduation. An education for a traditional profession, like those listed above, remains very much in demand by students who know what they want to do as their life's work. But those students are in the minority. Because of technological advances over the past fifty years, we now have many more choices of study, which makes career selection increasingly difficult.

I submit that it is almost impossible—with the hundreds of possible job combinations available today in industry, commerce, and the public sector—for the majority of young people to make a valid career decision prior to entering college.

My recommendation to those of you who are unsure of what major to choose or are uncomfortable with the major you now have is this:

Major in liberal arts.

Liberal arts is the most flexible and the most versatile of all majors. It can be adapted to whatever career you ultimately enter. With a liberal arts background you will be able to interface with the broadest spectrum of educated people on their levels. This is especially important in a professional sales career.

Even as far back as 1948, we college students sometimes changed our majors midstream. I switched from engineering to music theory and composition as I entered my third year at UCLA.

In addition to being a full-time college student, I was a professional trumpet player, playing part-time in the movie studios, as well as with my own dance band two nights a week all over Los Angeles. I loved music, but I also loved aircraft engineering, so I played it safe: I kept engineering as my minor.

And it's a good thing that I did. When the music business fizzled in the late 1940s, thanks to the advent of television, I ended up taking an engineering job. My employer, Northrop Aircraft, allowed me to complete my engineering credentials at night while working days as a trainee. But if I hadn't already had a college degree—*even one in music*, as mine was—I never would have been given that opportunity.

After six years as an aerospace engineer, I again switched gears, this time into professional sales, selling high-tech products to the aerospace industry. I mention this only to show how we often end up taking a roundabout route to our true life's work.

What is important at this stage of life's game is that you receive a solid college education, the foundation upon which *you can build any kind of career you want*. Your college degree is your pass-key, your "admission to life" ticket that allows you the chance to learn and prove yourself in a variety of possible careers other than those directly related to your major.

What your degree means to most prospective employers is that you have the tenacity and ability to stick to something important and see it through to completion. From that point on, assuming you are entering the workforce, your employer will be your new college—paying you to learn what you need to know to perform whatever job you have been hired to do.

> **Today a college degree is your key to the inner sanctums of the worlds of business, commerce, and the public sector. If you don't have one, you are locked out.**

CHAPTER TWO

WHO ARE PROFESSIONAL SALESPEOPLE?

Professional salespeople are college graduates who sell goods and services to other professionals.

> I am *not* talking about retail sales. I *am* talking about commercial, industrial, and fund-raising sales.

I use the term "professional sales" to distinguish it as the absolute highest level of sales.

Professional salespeople are representatives of the most prestigious companies in the world, and they must be able to interact with the top echelons of industry, commerce, and the public sector. Their customers include lawyers, judges, colleges, universities, libraries, publishers, engineers, architects, chemists, chemical engineers, consultants, high-tech companies, accountants, scientists, distributors, research labs, medical practitioners, and similar professional enterprises.

Despite the fact that this job is based on professional-to-professional relationships, there are few schools that prepare an individual for a professional sales career.

Colleges Have Overlooked Sales as a Career

Sales is the least talked-about of all possible careers. It has long been assumed that sales is something people fall into, rather than something they train for. Traditionally companies have trained their own sales personnel because they have had no choice.

It seems to be the best-kept secret on campus. But that is understandable because there are no established sales curricula in any school that I know of, though that is about to change.

While at college, it seems as though sales does not exist, but out in the world, it *does* exist—big time! And this is ironic because most colleges and universities have full-time employees who are *professional salespeople*—specializing in one of the highest levels of professional sales—*fund raising*. They are not called salespeople. They don't even think of themselves as salespeople. They are professionals, usually with law degrees (tax law specialty) or business degrees (MBA or accounting), but make no mistake about it, their main job is *professional sales.*

Often these professionals are located around the country in populous regions. But the leader of this group is on campus, and may be officially known as the "Vice President of Institutional Development," or some other such title. This speaks well to the importance of their fund-raising activities. This group is the life's blood of most educational institutions. They call on alumni and other friends of the college, one-on-one, seeking contributions, investments, and sponsorships. This is what professional sales is all about: College graduates provide needed services (in this case, estate counseling) to other college graduates, and are then rewarded (with donations to or investments in their college).

These specialists hold estate planning seminars at many college events that wealthy alumni attend. These seminars are centered around Charitable Remainder Trusts, Charitable Annuities, Gift Giving, Estate Tax Planning, and a host of other alternatives, all designed to endow the college with huge sums of money in exchange for significant tax benefits and/or annuity income for the donors. As I said, this is one of the highest forms of sales, and it is how colleges and universities raise money over and above state and federal funding, if any. Harvard University has billions of dollars in private endowment reserves, all raised by professional salespeople who are employees of that university. This is where most scholarship money comes from, as well as funds for internships and other peripheral projects. Yes, professional sales is alive and well in academia.

Professional sales is more directly responsible for the success and maintenance of our free market, private enterprise economy than is *any other single element.* That is why professional sales pays so well. That is why it leads to top management positions faster than most other career paths.

Now this little book isn't intended to teach you the rudiments of selling. At last count in my local bookseller I found 129 "how-to" and "how-not-to" books on every aspect of selling. The titles included *Mistakes by Salesmen, Close Every Sale, 25 Best Habits, Presentations, Sales Letters, Selling Techniques, Trade Show Selling, Sales Skills, Relationship Selling, Superstar Sales Secrets, Fund Raising Sales,* and a host of others. I found most of them to be of value, although many say the same things in different ways. They are useful reference materials, both while you are learning and during your career as you encounter the inevitable challenges a first-class professional must anticipate, identify, and solve.

But no book can make you a seasoned professional salesperson. You must get experience. You must get your feet wet—and learn from your mentors.

Exciting Opportunities

What I am trying to do here is open your eyes to the fantastic array of exciting opportunities that await you in a professional sales career—provided you first become well-grounded and well-rounded academically. A bachelor's degree is a must. And, as I have said, while most majors will do, a strong liberal arts or general education background is preferred.

I want to stress that point: Liberal arts offers one of the *broadest* intellectual backgrounds of all disciplines. To communicate successfully with a wide variety of highly educated professional clients, top-level salespeople *must* have a broad range of general knowledge.

It is true that you don't need a degree to get into lower-level retail selling, but without one, at some point, your career will hit a dead-end.

> **Top-level sales and management jobs in the best institutions are reserved for those with a college education.**

That said, a good education alone is not enough: You must also have the right combination of aptitudes. I will discuss this in Chapter 4.

CHAPTER THREE

A RECESSION-PROOF CAREER? ABSOLUTELY!

When I was thinking about changing my career from aerospace engineering to professional sales—that is, to selling high-tech products and services to the aerospace industry—I realized I needed guidance. I needed someone to help me break into the exclusive field of professional sales. For one thing, I had no previous sales experience.

But I did have the good fortune to be referred to a Los Angeles sales consultant—C. B. Buchanan, the man to whom this book is dedicated.

For a fee, he worked with me privately one evening a week for about three months. He didn't teach me how to sell. No one can do that. But he taught me that learning to sell effectively comes from associating and working with successful salespersons, absorbing the best of their traits and habits, and reading about the sales experiences of renowned professional salespeople. C. B. stimulated my awareness, and gradually brought me to an understanding of why I felt compelled to be in sales, why I thought I could be successful, and how to select the best company with which to cast my lot as a sales-engineer trainee.

Unusual Background

Buchanan was a very interesting man. In his early years, during the Great Depression of the 1930s, he was employed by the state of California as a department manager of one of its employment offices. In those years the unemployment rate hovered around 30 percent, much higher than in any modern-day recession. C. B. noticed that while he rarely received employer requests for people to fill "regular" jobs, he always had a thick stack of requisitions for salespeople.

In those days the majority of sales jobs were "commission sales." That is, the salesperson received no salary, no paid expenses, no benefits; the pay was a percentage of the sale of products sold. Some of these jobs were selling door-to-door, which was very popular until about 1960. Those who were good at it and worked hard made more money during the Depression than most salaried middle managers did then.

This was the era of the famous "Fuller Brush Man." Fuller brushes were the gold standard of the household brush market—and they were *only* sold door-to-door. You couldn't buy a Fuller brush at the store. If Fuller didn't have a brush in its broad line, you didn't need it. Almost every housewife in America looked forward to her monthly visit from the Fuller Brush man, who always brought her a free sample. Similarly, Avon cosmetics also began its long-term success by door-to-door sales.

Challenge

What C. B. couldn't understand was why so few people would try their hands at selling during the Depression when so many were *dead broke and needed work.* There were few, if any, unemployment benefits or safety nets in those days. It was either sponge off your relatives and friends or stand in bread lines and eat at soup kitchens.

Compelled to research this curious fact, C. B. quit his job with the employment office—which took a lot of fortitude during those tough years, especially with a family to support—and sought a job in sales. Although he, too, had no previous sales experience, he selected one of the most exclusive companies in the country as his target employer. The company was Remington-Rand (now known as UNISYS), the huge business machine, typewriter, and business systems innovator. In those days it was bigger than IBM.

He chose Remington-Rand because he had used its accounting and personnel systems while working for the state and so was already familiar with its products. Nonetheless, getting the job *was* a big job. And here is a prime example of what persistence can do for you. It took him 30 straight working days of calling on the same local R-R sales manager to land a job as a sales trainee. The manager told him: "Buchanan, if you work as hard selling for me as you did selling me on giving you this job, you will be the best man in my district." And he was. Over the years, C.B. had a very successful career in commission sales, eventually becoming a salaried district manager.

The Entrepreneurial Instinct

During his later years with Remington-Rand, C.B. grew increasingly intrigued by the wide variations in his salesmen's personalities and work habits, and in the company's attitudes about and methods of sales training. As his interest in selling and managing diminished, he opted to leave R-R to start his own sales consulting business. His consulting activities included the contract training of sales forces—and the training of individuals like me.

I don't know that he ever solved the mystery of why so few people would try sales during the Great Depression, though he did learn a lot about recruiting and motivating salesmen.

My personal theory is that the vast majority of people are afraid to have anyone say "no" to them. They perceive "no" as a personal rejection, which in sales isn't the case at all! Not everyone will buy your product or service for any number of reasons—oftentimes for reasons totally unrelated to you, your company, or the products you represent.

Because professional sales relationships develop naturally over time, they lead naturally, almost automatically, to sales. Hard facts and *mutual benefits* are paramount in these business relationships; emotions are seldom involved. Consequently, at the professional level of sales, you rarely hear the word "no" at all.

And unlike the old days, commission sales jobs are very rare. Today professional salespeople are generally paid a good salary with a car allowance, an expense account, and a generous bonus for meeting and exceeding sales projections.

Sales Overcomes Recessions

The main lesson in this chapter is that no matter how bad times are, there is always a demand for professional salespeople. This includes lower-level sales as well, as shown by C. B. Buchanan's experience with the California employment office during the Depression. It always applies to the middle and highest levels of professional sales.

In fact, employers scale up their searches for more effective salespersons during a recession. When business is recessive, sales and marketing efforts must be substantially increased. Why? Because that is how businesses survive recessions! Sales in general and professional sales in particular run counter to business downturns: Professional sales never experiences a recessive cycle of its own.

Remember my first law of business reality:

There is rarely anything wrong with any company that more sales won't cure.

CHAPTER FOUR

WHAT IS PROFESSIONAL SALES?

When I talk about sales to young people I am invariably asked, "Well, besides car salesmen, telemarketers, and the clerks at Wal-Mart, who else is in sales?" My answer invariably is, "Just about everbody." Some of the greatest natural-born salespeople I have encountered are college presidents and vice presidents, corporate CEOs, classroom teachers, managers at all levels, and non-profit foundation solicitors.

After all, what is sales? **Sales is persuasion.**

Since we no longer manage by decree, the most successful managers have to be superb salespeople. They must be able to persuade colleagues and subordinates to consent to comply with their leadership. Today's employees are far too sophisticated to be ordered or bullied into doing anyone's bidding.

Extracting money from people, even for the most noble purposes, is one of the most artistic forms of persuasion. In its best form, the giver actually enjoys being part of the process.

Following my retirement at age forty-six from the corporate world of sales, marketing management, and being president and CEO of two high-tech companies, I entered politics. Subsequent to my election to the Nevada State Legislature, I was appointed vice chairman of Ways and Means—the money committee—and chairman of the Committee on Higher Education Funding. I battled extensively with university and community college presidents and a battalion of Ph.D. department heads over budgets and other matters.

During my tenure in that venerable institution—and, out of habit, always on the lookout for extra-special sales talent—I made a study of the sales techniques *used on me* by the members of academia. They were some of the most persuasive and tenacious natural-born salespeople I have ever seen! I was in awe of them. Yet when I jovially referred to my academic friends as superb salespeople, they recoiled in horror! The thought of being compared to a salesperson was, to them, undignified. They didn't understand that professional sales calls for a combination of knowledge, wisdom, planning, preparation, and psychology seldom matched in other careers. To my mind it was one of the highest compliments I could pay.

A Wealth of Opportunities

Let's face one fact, whether we are aware of it or not, every day of our lives we are surrounded by all sorts of people who are trying to sell us all sorts of things, even if it is only an idea.

Some of the common, and not-so-common, sales careers awaiting you are in the fields of insurance, finance, stocks and bonds, custom software, aerospace and other high-tech products, engineering services, pharmaceuticals, medical equipment and supplies, building contracting, manufacturing, tourism, conventions, retail stores, banking services, hotel services, seminar services, health spas, sports services, entertainment, food and beverage industries, consulting, real estate, advertising, publishing, public relations, aircraft sales and leasing, transportation, janitorial supplies and services, freight forwarding, automobiles and the automobile industry, lobbying and fund raising—just to name a few.

Companies and institutions serving these markets employ either full-time salespeople or contract sales representatives, sales reps.

Every last one of these employers is always actively seeking better educated salespersons.

Greatest Economic Opportunity

For those who are qualified, a professional sales career provides the greatest economic opportunity available within a free market economy.

While there are many earnings levels in sales, the best educated and truly professional sales practitioners consistently earn higher salaries and bonuses than do other employees in most companies. They often exceed the earnings levels of the licensed professions.

Why is sales such a high paying profession? Because salespeople are the self-starters on the firing line—the internal entrepreneurs, if you will—whose successes or failures determine if a company's planned projections will or will not be met.

The accounting, finance, procurement, human resources, engineering, and manufacturing operations of a business—while conducting vital functions involved with producing *what has already been sold by the sales department*—are not the prime movers.

Sales, with support from marketing, determines what tomorrow's products and services will be.

As the venerable Red Motley, crowned the world's greatest salesman by his peers back in the early 1950s, always said:

> **"Nothing happens until somebody
> sells something."**

For example, not a single automobile is produced until it has been pre-sold to a dealer. Think back through the process of what goes into building a car—from the manufacture of steel, to the design and manufacture of each component, to the transport of parts to the assembly line—and you can see that a whole lot happens once that auto is sold. In fact, it's staggering.

All product and commodity production is based upon *projections of anticipated sales*—and the salespeople make those projections. Everything else follows. Sales is the front line, the prime mover. Its failures and successes, and the failures and successes of each individual salesperson, are visible for all to see.

Those who don't meet projections don't last very long. But for those who do, the aesthetic and material rewards are the very best. The beauty of sales is that you always get credit for your own successes or failures, and are rewarded commensurately.

Wide Latitude

Therefore, professional sales isn't for the faint-hearted. To be successful, you must be an energized self-starter with the desire to win, to stand as an individual risk-taker—you must think and feel like an entrepreneur.

Salespeople have a lot of latitude to operate within the company envelope. They do their own planning, their own scheduling, they write their own reports, make their own forecasts, adjust their own working hours to accommodate their customers, entertain customers as necessary, and generally operate without supervision, provided, of course, they stay within the bounds of company policy.

While most sales managers do stand ready to teach, assist, and support their salespeople, they *do not* micromanage. Micromanaging salespeople kills incentive and creativity. There is a delicate balance here between effective and ineffective sales management.

Aesthetic Rewards

I don't want to give you the impression that monetary rewards are the most important part of a successful sales career. Far from it! As the noted behavioral expert

Friedrich Herzberg proved many years ago, "Money is a dissatisfier."

No one is, or ever will be, completely satisfied with the amount of money that he or she makes or has. It is basic human nature to always want more—for the kids' education, for the unforeseen rainy day.

But it has been proven again and again that genuine career satisfaction isn't tied to money. As I always told my own offspring, who are well-educated and contentedly successful in their respective careers: "Career success is more accurately measured by how enthusiastic you are about going to work in the morning (or whenever)." Money is definitely second to contentment and achievement. Notice that I shun the word "happy." I have yet to meet anyone who maintains a blissfully happy state while at work. Satisfaction and contentment are enough.

Aptitudes

I'm sure you noticed that early on I referred to certain skills and "aptitudes" a successful sales professional must have. How do you know if you have what it takes to be a successful sales professional?

I know an excellent way to find out. The Human Engineering Laboratory* has been isolating and identifying the innate aptitudes of thousands of people for eighty-two years. This is not voodoo science.

Dr. Johnson O'Connor was an electrical engineer at General Electric in 1920 when he was assigned the task of finding out why some assemblyline workers could use their fingers in a dexterous manner, but couldn't use small tools, and vice versa. He developed a series of dexterity tests that answered that question, which led to his identifying and solving other aptitude problems for the company.

In 1922, he left GE to found The Johnson O'Connor Research Foundation, which soon became known as the Human Engineering Laboratory. He also helped to develop psychomotor tests that were used by the U.S. Army Air Corps during WWII to determine who could be a pilot or a bombardier or a navigator. I took those tests prior to entering my pilot training.

_____

*Human Engineering Laboratory, Inc., 347 Beacon Street, Boston, MA 02116; 800.355.3670. There are branch offices in Atlanta, Chicago, Dallas/Ft. Worth, Denver, Houston, Los Angeles, New York, San Francisco, Seattle, and Washington, D.C.

The Lab's data bank contains the aptitude test results of thousands of *eminently successful* people from all walks of life. When we are tested by the Lab, our aptitudes are compared to theirs. *Success* is the norm at the Lab, not national averages.

I strongly recommend that everyone take the entire battery of tests—as did my children when they were teenagers, and as I had many years before.

While only three or four tests are needed to verify basic sales aptitude, your other aptitudes will help determine what you should—and should not—be selling. Should you be selling tangibles—equipment, pharmaceuticals, software, real estate—or intangibles—securities, insurance, advertising, consulting, fund raising? Your combined aptitudes will determine that.

But first and foremost, it is vital to identify your "personality" type, which is your most important "aptitude," no matter what career you pursue. It is noteworthy that the same personality aptitude that is a *must* requirement for a long-term, successful professional sales career is identical to the ideal aptitude for managers and classroom teachers.

Yes, it is possible to succeed in sales with the "wrong" personality aptitude—for a short time. But such misplaced people burn out quickly. They become agitated and no longer want to deal with clients, or people in general.

I am not talking about introversion versus extroversion, which relate to the groups we are in at any given time. That is, I can be an extrovert in group A and an introvert in group B. The personality aptitude goes much deeper than that.

It is absolutely essential that you know if you should be working with and through people or working alone, isolated from much human contact. You may think you already know the answer to that question without being tested, but I assure you that you do not. Your personality test outcome will not be influenced in the least by your feelings about people at any given time. Those moods are changeable—your personality is not!

One more very important thing. The Lab's battery of aptitude tests does *not* take your interests into consideration. Many so-called aptitude tests, popular with many colleges and universities, are little more than interest or psychological profiles.

All of us have one or two latent aptitudes that need to be discovered. We also have interests in areas where we have little or no aptitude. Witness music and art, for example, which are among the more abused examples of high interest/low aptitude.

For career success and emotional stability, it is important that you *develop your strongest aptitudes* and not waste time on pursuits where your aptitudes are weak. Forewarned is forearmed!

Once you discover a hitherto untapped aptitude, believe me, you will become fascinated with it and interested in developing that aptitude in your work and play.

> **Know your real abilities. Let your competitors wonder about theirs.**

By the way, these Human Engineering Lab tests were responsible for my leaving aerospace engineering in favor of sales engineering—professional sales. From that moment, I became a whole person, and my career accelerated beyond my wildest dreams.

College Dropouts

A primary reason many students drop out of college is that although they have the natural aptitudes, the energy level, and the drive for professional sales, *they just don't know it!* Without direction, they are restless and often bored with school.

The college environment is too confining for most natural-born salespeople because the long periods of isolation (studying) conflict with their inherent need for more than average social intercourse.

If you fail to see a direct connection between your college major and an exciting career, you become frustrated. You want to drop out of school and get a job (doing what?), which is really dumb!

Ironically, the odds are that if you drop out, you will probably end-up in a lower-level sales job because that is where you can make the most money. Given the choice, some companies will hire sales trainees with some college over those with no college.

> **There is no question that college dropouts are dead-ended careerwise early in the game. No exceptions!**

If there is a good chance that you will end up in sales anyway, why not remain in school and do it right? Get your degree and become a genuine professional salesperson. The sky is the limit.

No Matter What You Decide . . .

Perhaps after reading this far, you have already decided against a career in professional sales. By all means, *be tested by the Human Engineering Laboratory anyway*. I can't stress this enough.

Make sure you really belong in whatever career you do choose. Far too many of us have *some* of the aptitudes required for success in our chosen career, but we don't have the *right combination* to achieve our goals. We work hard, struggling along with less than satisfying results. Others pass us by with seemingly little effort.

I assure you, however, that if your aptitudes *are* suitable for professional sales, that you get your college degree, and that you are a hard-working individual who isn't afraid to stand on your own, there will be no stopping you from being highly successful. Once you learn how to break into this wonderful exclusive profession, that is.

CHAPTER FIVE

APPLYING FOR A PROFESSIONAL SALES JOB

No matter how good a company's products or services may be, they can't do any good until they have been sold to an end user.

Let me give you an example. My first company was a high-tech engineering and manufacturing company that started with little or no money, but we had a great new idea for pH measurement and control. We made an astounding technical breakthrough, revolutionizing pH measurement. Now that we had it, what to do with it?

Naturally, you would think that chemical companies, oil refineries, food processors, and distillers—all dependent upon pH control—would beat a path to our door, take these instruments away from us, and shower us with money, right? Wrong! They didn't know about us. We didn't have the money to advertise, and nobody would have believed our "outrageous" claims anyway. For thirty years, the pH market had been owned by three companies: Beckman Instruments, Foxboro, and

Leads & Northrup, all giants. Somehow we had to get our Cinderella story told—and believed.

The only option open to us was to *sell, sell, sell.* Two of my partners and I traveled around the country for months, taking red-eye specials (after-midnight flights that were cheap), and sleeping in flea-bag motels, carrying our pH instruments for demonstration purposes. Our targets were the chief engineers of Texaco, Shell, ARCO, Chevron, Monsanto, Union Carbide, Dow Chemical, Union Oil, Phillips, Conoco, and many others. This is what *professional sales* is all about! We were college graduates and we were calling on college graduates.

Our sales pitch was very simple. We offered the engineers a trial program: They could use our instruments *free of charge* for ninety days. We urged them to shake-down our pH instruments in as many diabolical ways as they could think of, in the worst environments they could dream up. If our instruments didn't outperform every other pH instrument they had ever used or seen, they could just return them to us—post-collect.

On the other hand, if our instruments proved to be as superior as we claimed, they could keep the demonstrators and send us a check. Not one instrument was returned. Over time we got enough checks to be able to afford first-class advertising.

In three short years we went from obscurity to number one in pH measurement and control. We dominated the market, and still do. You can see that there is no way the Internet could have sold our products to those chief engineers. These sales came from one-on-one presentations of the highest caliber. Our pH instruments saved each of our customers millions of dollars in a few years' time, and those sales made us millions of dollars in return. That is what you call *mutual benefits!* There is nothing like the thrill of solving a nasty problem for your customer—and then getting a big purchase order or contract in return.

And again, no matter how much it is touted as the answer to our sales and marketing prayers, the Internet can't do the job. *The Internet sells nothing!* It *merchandises* wares in the same way a store window does—but it doesn't *sell* them because there are no live salespeople. Nine times out of ten you already know what you want before you do a Web search. What you are really searching for is the best price and availability. That is not sales: That is merchandising, and it is very limited in service options.

If a company has wares that can be sold online, without people-interface, then it is most fortunate. Its cost of sales will be very low. But in the real world, in the world of *professional-level sales*, one-on-one, face-to-face, eyeball-to-eyeball people-interface is *vital*.

It takes real, live people to understand and articulate the advantages and special features of a company's products and to *persuade the customer to choose your product* and not your competitor's.

Mutual Benefit

While sales may be the art of persuasion, it is mostly a service through which professional salespeople do good for others and themselves by creating opportunities and situations that result in *mutual* benefit.

For a sales relationship to be worthy of the term "relationship"—meaning ongoing, sustained interaction—it must benefit your customer as much as it benefits your company and yourself. In a professional sales setting you are in the middle, representing the *best interests of both your customer and your company.* Ultimately this benefits you as well, aesthetically and financially.

Selling merely to enhance one's own financial gain will not work in the long term. Salespeople with money as their sole motivation burn out early.

This is why many car salespeople don't last very long. They focus only on selling a car *now*, as quickly as possible, with little or no regard to building a customer base for tomorrow's sales. The most successful auto salespeople I know, the ones who are my friends—and in particular the one who was indirectly responsible for my having founded my first high-tech company—do think about ongoing customer relationships. They plan for the future, which is why they end up being the managers, and often the owners, of dealerships.

Choosing the Right Company

The first thing you need to do is identify the companies with which you would want to work. This is where your *interests* and *other aptitudes* come into play. What products and/or services would you feel comfortable representing? What products or services are closely identified with your education, experience, and interests?

This is very important. While the company that hires you will train you in the proper application and use of its products, there is a definite advantage in selling products and services that you already have some knowledge of or interest in.

It is *essential* that you believe in the need for the products or services that you sell.

Getting an Interview

Let's say you have decided to see if you can land a good entry-level sales trainee job with a first-class company. However, you have no sales experience.

You've made a short list of companies that produce and/or distribute products that are to your liking and that you can believe in, products that are within your frame of reference—in other words, products you would feel good selling.

You happen across a newspaper ad for college graduate sales *trainees*, and note that the ad was placed by a company you would be proud to represent. In this situation getting an interview will be simple. Just follow the instructions in the ad.

However, it is highly unlikely that a top-flight company would advertise for professional-level salespeople, or college graduate trainees, in this manner, although I suppose it could happen.

For the sake of this exercise, let's say that you haven't seen any ads for salespeople and that you have no personal contacts that could secure your entrée into the company of your choice.

You've decided instead to take the "cold call" approach to getting an interview. In your mind this would be wonderful, if you can pull it off.

First, you have to get an interview with the home office sales manager, or a regional or local sales manager. Unlike law firm recruiters or, say, pharmaceutical company recruiters who regularly visit campuses in search of worthy prospective employees, sales managers rarely do that.

Colleges traditionally do not offer courses in sales—nor do they encourage sales careers in other ways—so sales managers feel there is little point in interviewing students who have never even been exposed to the possibility of a sales career. As professional salespeople themselves, they know their audience. They know where to put their energy to receive the best results.

The Old-Fashioned Approach

Let's take a look at what typically happens when you cold-call a regional or district sales manager.

First you have to get through the receptionist, and then perhaps the secretary, who will want to know the purpose of your call. If neither know of any immediate sales job openings, they may cut you off right then and there.

Should you manage to get through to the sales manager, the odds are that you will be told there are no job openings at that particular time (especially for an inexperienced sales trainee). Rarely will any sales manager take the time to interview a prospective hire if no position is in the offing. These people are simply too busy.

You may be asked to send in a resume. However, be advised that if you do, it will likely die a file-drawer death unless you follow up and call back weekly.

Reread Chapter 3 and note what C. B. Buchanan did to get his sales job with Remington-Rand. Remember that while sales is persuasion, it is also *perserverance.* As an applicant for a sales job, you are expected to be persistent. It should be obvious that this is what sales managers are looking for. Determination! Enthusiasm! Those who exhibit these traits will not only get the jobs, they will be successful at them.

It's ironic, but I am sure that within a short time of your unsuccessful attempt to get an interview with that sales manager, a job will open up for a sales trainee. But will that sales manager check the resume file and call you up? No. To a sales manager, anyone who has submitted a resume that is over one month old but hasn't made any follow-up attempts isn't worth having.

So if you do elect to do this the hard way—the old-fashioned way—by directly contacting regional or local sales managers, keep in contact! Call back or visit their offices every week.

Unless you can impress upon the sales manager how much you really want the job, he or she will take the easy route and hire an experienced salesperson away from a competitor. Although this costs more salarywise, there is little or no training involved. Realize you are facing an uphill battle.

To restate: When looking for a sales job *never send a resume until your interview is scheduled.* The only exception to this might be if the home office sales manager or the vice president of sales personally requests it.

And remember: *Follow up. Follow up. Follow up.*

Lots of luck.

The Innovative Approach

To my thinking, you should *avoid* making direct contact with a company's sales or regional sales manager. Yes, you read me correctly. The following has proven to be the most effective method for me and for the many others I've helped launch into sales careers.

Do your research, find out where your chosen company's home office is, and get the full name and address of the president or CEO or general manager.

Then compose a short, concise letter—not an email, an actual letter—to *one of them* requesting an interview for a sales job. Briefly mention your enthusiasm for the company and its products, and tell them you are a recent college graduate with a high energy level, who is eager to learn. You might even go so far as to suggest that perhaps somewhere within the company there is an underperforming salesperson who should be replaced.

That will most assuredly bring a chuckle or two. You audacity may be momentarily resented, but you perspicacity will be appreciated.

Your letter must be grammatically correct and clean, with zero errors and no erasures. Keep it short. Make it perfect.

And pay attention to my four "DON'Ts."

1. Don't *ever* use the word "position" in your letter. You want a JOB, not a position.

2. Don't enclose your resume with the letter. You will be asked to bring that with you when you report for your interview.

3. Don't mention that you have no previous sales experience.

4. Don't give your college major *unless* it in some way directly ties to the company's products or services.

Remember, the only objective of this letter is to get your foot in the door, to get you an interview. You don't want to prejudice anyone's thinking one way or another in advance of that interview.

Are you doing this to attract attention? To stand out from the crowd? Well, yes, of course you are. But, as you will soon learn, that is not the main reason for taking this approach to getting an interview.

Using the Innovative Approach

The surest and simplest way to get a job interview is to send your letter to one of the top guns in the company—either the CEO, the president, or the general manager.

Your letter will then be forwarded to the home office sales manager. That person will know (1) if there are any sales trainee openings, and (2) where they are. He or she will forward your letter to the appropriate regional or local manager. If there are no immediate openings, your letter will be forwarded to the regional or local sales manager closest to you.

Either way you will be interviewed. This will happen partly because your letter came down from the top. But it will happen mostly because of your initiative: Sales managers are curious about imaginative sales applicants. And in comparison to most applicants, your letter approach to getting an interview *is* imagi-native—and innovative.

If during your interview you are asked why you sent your letter to the CEO or general manager, merely reply that you thought the home office would best know which area of the country has an immediate opening. Tell them you are willing to relocate: Being willing to relocate is a huge plus.

And now on to the interview.

CHAPTER SIX

SURVIVING THE INTERVIEW AND GETTING THE JOB

Your interview will be your first selling job for that company: That is, you will be selling yourself to them. It won't be easy.

Professional sales managers for top companies only want the best people on their staffs. During an interview, they play hardball. Keep in mind that if a selling job for this company is really worth having, your interviewer will resort to every trick in the book to unnerve you, to see how you react to the unexpected under pressure.

Do not expect special treatment because you are a young, inexperienced recent graduate. The fact that you have no previous sales experience will incline your interviewer to be even harder on you. He or she will want to see how you overcome that disability.

You will do that by presenting yourself well, and by having a good, positive, and confident interview.

On the other hand, if your interviewer doesn't appear concerned about your lack of sales experience, then you should take a second look at the company before signing on. If it is too easy, there is something spooky about the job they intend to give you.

Now I am going to let you in on a secret that will help you significantly during your interview. It has to do with knowing your audience, your market, which in this case is the sales manager/interviewer.

Sales managers, salespeople in general, are sitting ducks for other good salespeople. We can't help it. It is our Achilles heel. We dearly love being persuaded by the best. During your interview, keep in mind that your interviewer *wants* to be sold on you.

But you need to be prepared.

Your Appearance

Before we talk more about the interview itself, let's discuss how you are going to dress for the occasion.

Remember, your college days are over. You are about to enter the big leagues. If you think you can get away with typical college attire for a professional sales interview, you had better limit your job applications to *Rolling Stone* or the blogosphere.

It's not because professional salespeople are stiff-necked prudes that we insist on a dress code. We like to let our hair down just like everyone else. But we know that *first impressions count.* If you are going to be a professional salesperson you are going to be in the business of making good first impressions.

Professional salespeople have customers and *prospective* customers to consider. We cannot afford to risk losing even one contract or purchase order by offending a client by our appearance. So dress with the odds.

What odds, you ask?

If you are a male, the odds are you won't offend anyone by NOT having a beard. The odds are you won't offend anyone by NOT having a pony tail. The odds are you won't offend anyone by NOT having multiple (visible) piercings. And the odds are you won't offend clients by wearing a well-tailored suit, a sports coat with slacks, or a dress shirt with a tie.

If you have a problem with these "odds," then you shouldn't consider a job in sales—unless you find a niche where your customers dress like rock stars or Hell's Angels.

If you are a female, the odds are the same, with some variations. You will want to dress conservatively, and by that I mean no low-cut dresses or blouses. No mini-skirts, either, whether part of a suit or not. Your interviewer doesn't want to be distracted by anything sexy; and if your interviewer is female, chances are she will be more critical of your dress than a male interviewer.

If you have a penchant for revealing or provocative clothing, limit your job interviews to companies like Fredericks of Hollywood or Victoria's Secret. In short, choose well-cut business suits with high-necked blouses and little or no jewelry.

Remember, as a salesperson, you will be representing the company. To the outside world, to your clients, you *are* the company! Don't think your interviewer won't be judging your appearance.

Interview Preparation

As I've said, your interview will not be easy, so be prepared. Here are a few questions you can expect to be asked.

Question 1: Why do you want a career in sales?

Assuming you pass the appearance test, one of the first questions you are likely to be asked is "Why do you want a career in sales?"

This is the most important question you could possibly be asked. If you paid attention to Chapter 4, you already know the answer.

If you say something like, "I want to sell because I like people," you are dead. Pick up your marbles and go home because there is no response worse than that one. In sales, you are expected to like people, just as you are expected to wear shoes and socks.

By far the most important reason you should want a career in professional sales is this:

> **Professional sales offers the greatest economic opportunity in a free market society.**

Period!

If that isn't your prime motivation, then, again, forget sales as a career.

The only other valid reasons for wanting a professional sales career is that you are a self-starter, that you are highly motivated to win, and that you love the idea of standing alone on your individual record. This is not to imply that you aren't a team player. Team work is important to a sales force, but within that group you want to be judged—win or lose—by your own efforts as an individual performer.

Question 2: What makes you think you can sell?

Since you have no previous sales experience, the next sticky question will probably be: "What makes you think you can sell?"

To answer this, you must do some serious self-evaluation. You, and only you, know what your most positive attributes are: your ability to persuade, your energy level, your desire to win, your ability to stick to a plan, to follow through, your self motivation. And how do you react to the unexpected? What other positives describe you as a person?

Remember, the interviewer wants to be sold on you. This is no time for either false modesty or braggadocio: It is the time for a calm, clear, concise presentation of your attributes.

Question 3: What makes you think you are qualified to sell our products?

The next question you should logically expect is: "What makes you think you are qualified—or can become qualified—to sell our products or services?"

To answer this, you must have done your homework. Well before the interview, get your hands on the company's brochures. Learn as much as you can about its products and services. Find out where its markets are.

Study these materials at home and develop your own sales presentation for one or two of the company's products. Practice in front of a mirror and on your family and friends. I suspect that if you give a brief, convincing sales presentation during the interview, you might well bring tears to your interviewer's eyes. Well, maybe I'm exaggerating, but you will be scoring some serious points. Sales managers just do not expect applicants with no sales experience to be that resourceful. The company may hire you even if there are no immediate openings! They may create a job for you rather than risk losing you to a competitor.

Other Tips and Considerations

Think before you speak, but don't hesitate too long when responding to a question. Some years ago, I interviewed a Stanford graduate. This was at a time when smoking a pipe was the cool thing to do. After I had asked this young man a key question, he paused and took out his pipe. He scraped the contents of the pipe bowl into my ashtray, and filled it with fresh tobacco, carefully tamping it down. Then he lit the pipe, took a long, thoughtful drag, and proceeded to respond. He didn't get the job.

Listen at every opportunity. If your interviewer starts talking about his or her own sales experiences, be attentive. You will learn something, and perhaps you won't have to dwell on your own lack of experience.

Don't allow yourself to get rattled, no matter what happens.

Remember that you are just as fussy about the company you select to work for as that company is when it selects you. Relay the fact that the integrity of the products and services you will represent is important to you.

If you handle these basic questions with confidence, poise, and a positive attitude, you will most likely be offered a good entry-level job in professional sales. Keep in the back of your mind that nearly all sales managers harbor a fantasy about discovering brilliant new sales talent. All you need to do is convince your interviewer that the brilliant new sales talent is you.

THE MOST GOOD FOR THE GREATEST NUMBER

So now you know the basics of breaking into professional sales as your new career.

When you think about it, it all comes down to common sense, which, as we all know, isn't all that common.

Putting yourself in your interviewer's shoes will reveal what he or she is looking for in you. The same holds true in professional sales. Put yourself in your customers' shoes and you will earn—and keep—their confidence.

I can't say this enough:

> **Professional sales is one of the most aesthetically rewarding and materially lucrative of all career opportunities in our society.**

It unquestionably *does the most good for the greatest number of people.* It provides the money for employers to pay their employees' salaries, commissions, and bonuses. It provides the money for R&D to do the work that assures the company's future. It provides the money for new equipment, machinery, and vehicles. It provides the money for new buildings and facilities. It provides the money for employee medical and retirement benefits. It provides the money for community and charitable contributions. And it provides the money for federal, state, county, and city taxes.

Professional sales is *the* prime mover.

Because, as you now know:

> **"Nothing happens until somebody sells something."**

I wish you well.

ABOUT
THE
AUTHOR

Bob Thomas is the author of *The Fail-Proof Enterprise: A Success Model for Entrepreneurs*, which is used as a reference text by colleges and universities in business management classes and entrepreneurial seminars.

Raised and educated in Long Beach, California, he served as an aviation cadet in the U.S. Army Corps during the latter part of WWII. He later graduated from UCLA, and worked as an aerospace engineer for six years before entering the field of high-tech product sales and marketing, where he soon became a sales and marketing manager.

Following seven years in sales and marketing, he founded, and was first president and CEO of, UNI-LOC, a high-tech electronic instrumentation company serving the oil, gas, chemical, and petrochemical industries. Today UNI-LOC is known as Rosemount Analytical, a division of Emerson Process (formerly Emerson Electric), a Fortune "500" company.

A few years after retiring from UNI-LOC he founded, and was first president and CEO of, TBI (Thomas-Barben Instruments), also a high-tech instrumentation company, which was sold to Bailey Controls–McDermott, another Fortune "500" company. It is now a division of ABB, the Swiss high-tech conglomerate.

Thomas lives in Carson City, Nevada, where he owns Comstock Aviation and founded the Carson City Airport Authority. He served four years on the Carson City School Board, three terms as a Nevada legislator, and many years on governor-appointed boards. He just completed his twenty-first year of public service.